CREATIVE STENCILLING

techniques and templates

j e a n - m i c h e l   f e y - k i r s c h

Michael O'Mara Books Limited

First published in Great Britain in 1998 by
Michael O'Mara Books Limited
9 Lion Yard
Tremadoc Road
London SW4 7NQ

A CIP catalogue record for this book is available from the
British Library

ISBN 1-85479-345-4

1 3 5 7 9 10 8 6 4 2

Typeset by K DESIGN, Winscombe, Somerset
Printed and bound in Italy

C O N T E N T S

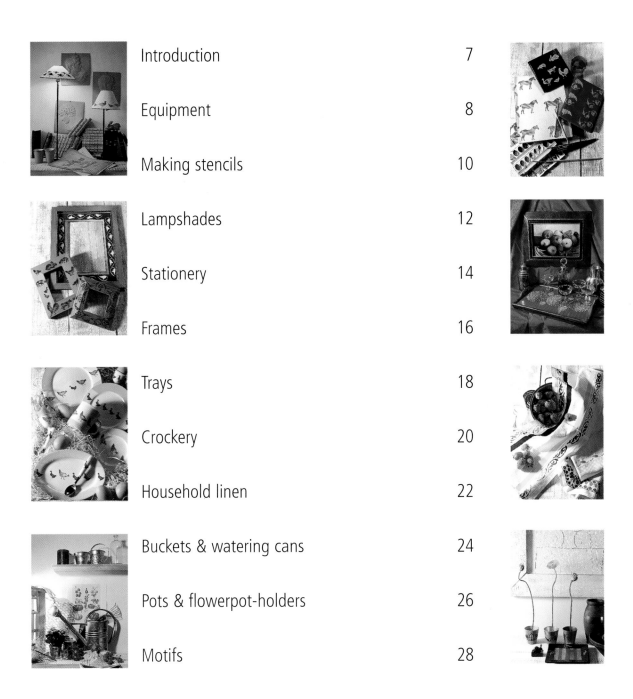

INTRODUCTION

The process of stencilling dates back to Antiquity. By its very nature, it allows you accurately to reproduce the same motif over and over again. Stencils can be simple or complex and the art of using them can be mastered by anyone.

This decorative technique is very flexible. It will make it easy for you to create friezes, patterns or scenes on a very wide range of surfaces: wood, fabric, paper, cardboard, metal, terracotta, porcelain, etc. You will therefore be able to decorate the objects in your home in the most surprising and charming ways.

In this book, you will find examples of items to decorate, instructions and tips, plus a selection of motifs that will help you to create your very own designs. All you need to do is to follow the technical instructions given in the first section, and to reproduce the motifs you have chosen from the many we have offered you in the second section, by tracing or photocopying them.

EQUIPMENT

Here is a list of the tools and equipment that will enable you to apply your stencils successfully to the medium you wish to use.

There's no need to buy all this equipment at once, just get what you need for the work you are doing.

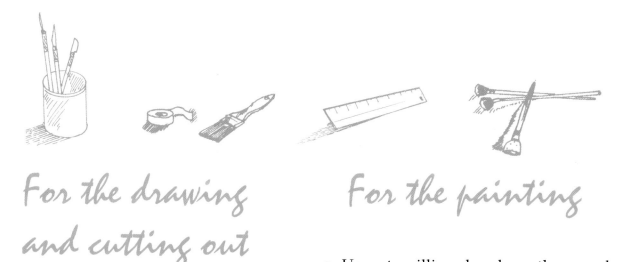

For the drawing and cutting out

- A grey HB 0.35 pencil

- A white rubber

- A ruler, preferably metal for cutting along with a blade

- A set square

- A roll of masking tape

- A craft knife

- A pair of scissors

- A scalpel with spare blades

- A piece of fibreboard or a sheet of glass (on which to cut out)

- Some tracing paper

- Some watercolour paper (light-weight 120–200g)

- Some watercolour or Ingres paper (heavy-weight, 300g and over)

- Some rhodoid for photocopying

For the painting

- Use stencilling brushes: the equal length of the hog-hair bristles makes it possible to cover surfaces evenly.

- Hog-hair graining brushes (flat-topped) in several widths

- A small sponge roller with spare rolls

- A kitchen sponge

- A small bottle of linseed oil that has been simmered in a bain-marie for 8 minutes from when the water boils. This makes it possible to waterproof stencils made out of watercolour paper by applying a coat on just one side of the stencil if you are using light-weight paper (200g), or on both sides if you are using thicker paper (300g or more).

- A spray-can of glue that allows repositioning (remount adhesive)

- A wire brush

- Some sheets of fine-grade sandpaper

- Small re-usable sticky notes

Paints

Different kinds of paint are suitable for different kinds of surface.

1 Oil paints need to be diluted with turpentine or white spirit. They are not used very much for stencilling because they take so long to dry. It is however possible to reduce the drying time by diluting the paint with matt varnish or acrylic varnish.

2 Acrylic paints are water-soluble and dry quickly to form an indelible plastic film. This enables you to apply several coats in quick succession. Brushes must be washed as soon as you have finished using them. They can also be soaked in water. If you allow them to dry, it becomes impossible to get the paint off them.

3 Fabric paints are sold in bottles or jars and can be used like watercolour paints. You must take care not to get too much on the brush because they are very runny and tend to flow under the stencil. Once the paint is dry, the design can be fixed onto the fabric by ironing over it, protected by a thin cloth. Once the paint is fixed, the item can be washed at a maximum of 60°C, but this can be risky.

4 Ceramic paints are difficult to use, not because they are tricky to handle, but because they often have to be fired at very high temperatures that cannot be reached using an ordinary domestic oven.

5 To protect your stencils more effectively, you can use cellulose paint of the one coat type, applied with a brush.

Patinas and varnish

- Gilder's bole. This brick-coloured substance is used as a base for gilding (on wood or pottery). You apply it with a cloth, a finger or a small brush.

- Antique dealers' gilding cream comes in a jar. You can rub it on with a cloth.

- Black patina comes in the same form as the gilding cream and can be applied using a cloth, your finger, or a fine brush.

- Crackle varnish

- Antiquing varnish

- Gloss varnish

- Matt varnish for oils

- Spray varnish

MAKING STENCILS

There are two steps to making stencils. The first consists of preparing and cutting out the motifs you have selected. The second consists of applying the paint to the object of your choice.

Several techniques for making your stencils

Cutting out stencils

1 Once you have chosen the motif, trace it onto some watercolour paper (about 220g) that you have already prepared with linseed oil. This weight of paper makes life easier if you are cutting out intricate motifs. For larger motifs you can use 300g paper.

2 You can of course use other materials, like sheets of rhodoid for example. However rhodoid requires careful handling because it is very fragile (it splits, wrinkles, etc.). You can photocopy your motif directly onto the rhodoid and then cut it out. (Acetate can also be used.)

3 It's also possible to photocopy your motif onto a sheet of paper, then tape the photocopy to some watercolour paper and cut out the two sheets together, to obtain your stencil.

When cutting out stencils, work either on a piece of wood or plywood, or on a sheet of glass. We recommend a sheet of glass which is easier to cut on. The blade slides more easily over the surface and doesn't dig into the material. Glass is also hard-wearing and retains a clean, smooth surface.

DON'T FORGET!

If you cut a simple motif out of your chosen material, you will obtain a stencil that can be used immediately. However if you are cutting out part of a complex motif, you need to create some 'bridges' on the design by which the various parts of the stencil can be held together (see the illustration on page 11).

Once you have cut out your stencil, allowing a sufficient number of regularly-spaced bridges depending on the design, you then need to protect your stencil if it is made out of watercolour paper, using cellulose paint. Once your stencil is dry and hardened by the paint, it is ready for use.

A few useful tips

- Your paint shouldn't be too runny or too dry.

- Practise on some paper before you embark on the real thing.

- It's more practical to pour some paint onto a plate or artist's palette, rather than to dip your brush directly into the paint-pot. This helps you to get the right amount of paint for the tool you are using and the effect you wish to create, and to work with a palette of colours, mixing them as required.

- Never overload your painting tool and dab the paint thinly over the stencil so that it does not run underneath.

- To prevent the stencil from slipping, it should be fixed in place with some masking tape. If the stencil is made of rhodoid, you can spray it underneath with some remount adhesive.

- Choose the appropriate tool for the type of stencil you are using:
  - A small graining brush for little, intricate motifs
  - Brushes or pads for larger designs
  - Rollers or sponges for creating different patinas.*

* Ageing technique used to give a surface a

bridge

11

By the light of the lamp … lampshades come into their own in the evening: by using transparent colours or startling contrasts, they can be decorated with bright ideas to light up your life!

1 On some A4-sized paper (21 × 29.7cm) draw in black a few simple motifs that are easy to cut out. Photocopy them onto a sheet of rhodoid, then cut them out with a craft knife or scalpel so that you can arrange them all around the lampshade. Measure the distance between each one so that you can space them evenly. Once you have decided where they will go, mark the position on the lampshade.

2 Position the stencils on the marks and fix them in place with masking tape. Pour some paint out into the pot lids or onto some saucers which will enable you to scrape your brush and control the amount of paint you are applying to the fabric. Apply the paint thinly using a flat-ended brush with very short, fine bristles. Allow plenty of time for it to dry so that you can be sure the paint doesn't run.

3 Remove the stencil and make sure it's quite dry before re-positioning it. To help your stencil to adhere to the fabric of the lampshade, you can spray the back of it with some remount adhesive. You can apply the paint very lightly or unevenly to give a 'worn' effect. You can produce a fainter motif by using a brush that is almost dry.

HANDY TIPS!

The conical shape of a lampshade is not very convenient for applying stencils, so make them small.

Painting stencils on a lampshade is quite tricky because fabric paint is rather runny and therefore more likely than other paint to stain surfaces.

Do not heat the lampshade to fix the paint.

Decorative stationery, whether it is subtle and discreet or flamboyant and adventurous, reflects the personality of its creator. Use stencils to liven up your mail, decorate your notebooks and delight everyone ...

1 First of all, you need a sheet of glass on which to cut out the stencils. Then choose the stationery items you want to personalise: writing paper and envelopes, diaries, notebooks, notepads, etc. You can even create your own albums and book-covers. To do this, you need some heavy-weight rag paper, watercolour paper or Ingres paper (200g or more).

2 Once you have decided what you are going to decorate, you can create a design using either a single stencil to match the size, or several smaller stencils that you can arrange however you like to make a pattern. Simple themes like animals, flowers or leaves can produce very attractive results because you can place them geometrically or at random.

3 Paint your stencil motifs using acrylic paint which is more pleasant to use, and very easy for blending colours. Use simple spacing and colour-schemes. When you are painting a porous substance like rag, watercolour, or Ingres paper, you don't need to apply a varnish. However on a notebook cover, for example, you can give it a shiny finish by simply applying a gloss varnish with a brush. Give the varnish plenty of time to dry then apply a second coat to even out the thicknesses of the paint.

HANDY TIPS!

It's great fun to make your own notebooks. You can simply hole-punch sheets of paper and bind them together with ribbon.

You can also sew the pages together using a big darning needle and some thick cotton thread or kitchen string to bind them. You can use rough or dainty stitching for a guaranteed artistic effect!

FRAMES

Every picture tells a story ... Scatter frames around your home to add an element of fantasy and familiar charm. They set off a smile or a captured expression, pictures of other places, the past and the present, and create a certain gentle nostalgia ...

1 As with stationery, there are several options open to you. If you want to create a varnished frame, you need to prepare the painting surface to make it non-porous, so that the varnish holds better. Sand the wood, apply an undercoat of primer, sand again, then apply the definitive shade of varnish. You can also leave the frame as it is and decorate a mount made of sticky-backed cardboard, to which you can apply your stencils.

2 Cut out a few little stencils and position them on the varnished frame. You can create different effects by applying your colour unevenly (see, for example, the frame decorated with animals) or dabbing on different colours with a brush (the frame decorated with clusters gives you an illustration). You can also use several fine brushes and different colours. Don't forget to attach your stencils to the frame with masking tape!

3 You can use either a matt or a gloss varnish. When your stencils are completely dry, use a small roller to apply a coat of varnish. Make sure the coat is evenly distributed and there are no air bubbles. Or, apply the varnish gently with a hog-hair brush, always smoothing it in the same direction.

HANDY TIPS!

Preferably, you should choose simple, flat frames. If there is a slant, the stencil is more difficult to position and blobs of paint are likely to form underneath.

To give your frame an 'aged' look, you can scrape it gently with a wire brush or some fine-grade sandpaper to lift off a bit of the paint in a few areas of the motif. Then varnish.

Rustic-looking for a picnic or stylishly decorated for a party, trays make life easy when moving everyday objects from place to place – from kitchen to bedroom, from garden to sitting room.

1 Measure the inside base of your tray and cut out a sheet of fairly heavy-weight (250g) smooth Bristol-board of the same size. You need it quite heavy so that it doesn't curl up once painted.

Trace a simple pattern on the Bristol-board using a ruler or pencil. You can use some masking tape or re-positionable tape as a frame if your drawing allows, so that you can paint without overflowing. Then prepare your acrylic paint on an improvised palette and paint your pattern. Allow to dry properly.

2 Mark out the position of your stencils with some re-usable sticky notes. If you have several little stencils or if you want to reproduce the same stencil several times, these will help you to place them accurately and won't leave any marks when they are removed.

If you are creating a large motif, paint your first colour from right to left, using a small pad brush. To create a graduated effect, only dip your brush into the colour once and allow the paint to run out as you reach the edge of the stencil. Leave to dry a second time.

You can then add some lustre by applying a second colour on top of the first, shading off in the opposite direction with a thin brush.

3 To give an aged appearance to your tray, use a crackle varnish. Once your motif is completely dry, give it two or three coats of water-based varnish in order to smooth out any areas of thick paint. Ensure that the varnish is evenly distributed over the whole surface of the motif. Allow to dry thoroughly between each coat.

Apply a first coat of crackle varnish, distributing it well in all directions using a hog-hair brush. Smooth it out, using the right amount of pressure. Leave to harden until the surface seems dry when you brush your finger over it. Apply a second coat. Don't forget that the more you allow the first coat of varnish to dry, the more successful the cracked effect will be. Allow ten days for the varnish to dry completely.

In order to emphasise the cracks, make a pad and apply some oil paint straight out of the tube (a sepia colour or a grey for example). Apply the paint from the pad using a circular motion, so that it gets into all the cracks. Very gently wipe off the surplus with a soft rag. Finally, stick your decorated paper onto the tray.

HANDY TIPS!

You can use some wallpaper on the bottom as a base, choosing a stripe or a plain or an imitation wood-grain in the colours of your choice.

Buy one or two tubes of oil paint. The colours are fabulous and the paint is easy to use.

You can age your tray in the same way as your design, which will make the whole thing look fantastic!

Fresh, country-style crockery which invites you to eat outside under the trees in the garden, or which summons you to a summer picnic in the shade of a patio parasol or in a meadow full of flowers.

1 You may need special equipment for firing ceramic paint, so you could replace it with food colouring which is less durable but which will enable you to recreate the design shown here quite easily. Two motifs, a duck and a hen, are used to create matching variations on a single theme. This technique of arranging two small motifs in a variety of ways can be used for all kinds of projects on all kinds of objects.

2 Draw and cut out your motifs from small sheets of rhodoid because the shape of crockery makes stencils difficult to apply. Use masking tape to trace the lines that will enable you to mark the exact position of the stencils. Stick your stencil onto the item to be stencilled and paint your motif. You can use a combination of different motifs or repeat the same one several times, using your own imagination. Then match your crockery by painting an identical band on the whole service using a roller.

HANDY TIPS!

To try your hand at crockery painting, why not buy a job lot of cheap white pottery to practise on.

If you use ceramic paint, you can have it fired in workshops equipped with kilns – you should find a list of them in the Yellow Pages. In this case, you can paint motifs on the inside of the crockery.

If you choose food colouring, restrict the decoration to the edge or the outside of the items, then protect it with a coat of varnish that is not water-soluble.

Fabrics of all kinds (cottons, linens, silks, etc.) can be used imaginatively to create atmosphere at your table, in your bedroom or your kitchen. With a swirl of patterns and colours, you can create cheerful and theatrical effects.

1 You can do anything with fabrics. Here are a few examples of how you can personalise your own household linen. To decorate towels and tea-cloths, you need to draw a motif that you can repeat several times, linking each one to the last to form a frieze. Trace it using a sheet of rhodoid and an indelible pen for plastics. Cut out the shape on a sheet of glass. It's an idea to make a spare because rhodoid is easy to cut, but it's rather flimsy and easily damaged.

2 Gently spray a bit of adhesive onto the back of your stencil and stick it to the fabric (remount adhesive doesn't stain). Dip a round brush lightly into the fabric paint and dab the motif, taking care to fill it in completely (each type of fabric will require a different amount of paint).

3 To emphasise your motif, you can create several friezes or perhaps add some coloured stripes. You can use one or several paints for your stencil. You can also create a graduated effect by starting with a light shade and gradually adding some darker colour as you work towards the centre. Then continue to dab on the dark colour, gradually eliminating the lighter colour until you obtain the dark colour on its own. You can of course work from light to dark or from dark to light. Make sure you rinse your brush regularly so that the colour changes rapidly. Leave the fabric to dry and then pass an iron over it to fix the colour, while protecting the motif with a cloth.

HANDY TIPS!

There are paints specially made for fabric-painting. They are fairly runny and therefore a bit tricky to handle. When applying them, put just a little on the brush and make sure that the stencil is stuck down firmly to the fabric.

Allow the paint to dry well before retouching or applying another colour.

Once you have finished you need to iron it, to help the paint to penetrate into the textile fibres. The heat of the iron should be regulated to suit the fabric.

Dry clean before washing for the first time.

BUCKETS & WATERING CANS

Nature clothes herself in green and gardens are overwhelmed by the exuberant growth of foliage and flowers. Toying with colour at the back of the shed, tools can be decorated to imitate the garden.

1 To help the paint to adhere to the metal surface you need to prepare it by lightly rubbing it down with some fine-grade sandpaper and applying a matt varnish. Then prepare your range of colours on a palette or a plate. Three or four shades will suffice. Allow a different brush for each of the colours. Prepare your stencil by spraying the back of it with some aerosol remount adhesive (it will adhere perfectly well for several paint applications). Once your varnish is dry, apply your stencil.

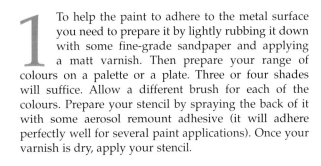

2 To be on the safe side, use some masking tape to stick on your stencil. You can give free rein to your imagination as you arrange your colours and blend the layers one after another without following any particular plan. The only precaution you must take is to allow the paint to dry properly between coats. You can start by applying the main colour with a pad. Then as you gradually get down to the fine detail, you will need thinner and thinner brushes.

3 You can repeat the same process several times by repositioning the stencil. Take care of course not to stick it onto a painted area, even if the paint is dry. For parts that are difficult to get at or when the main stencil cannot be used due to the curves, prepare some separate little stencils that will stick on more easily. This will prevent the paint from overflowing.

HANDY TIPS!

Choose acrylic paint from a tube but don't over-dilute it with water. Try to maintain a thick or medium consistency if your cut-outs are very intricate.

POTS & FLOWERPOT-HOLDERS

Beautiful clay colours blend well into any room. Soft and natural, or vibrant and colourful, they add a touch of warm comfort to your home.

1 Prepare some different stencils: arabesques, leaves, stripes, spots, etc. However keep the stencils small, as pots are normally conical in shape, making the stencils difficult to stick on. A bit of adhesive tape will help you.

You can create several effects: try a gold patina, for example, applied in two stages. Once you have fixed your stencil in place, first apply some gilder's bole with your finger or a small brush. Once it's dry, apply a gold patina on top with your finger and allow to dry. If you like, you can polish it and make it shine using a rag or a soft brush.

2 You can also use a black patina which is applied in exactly the same way as the brick-coloured gilder's bole. It is also possible to create a design with all three substances, using one, two or three at a time. Always allow the terracotta to absorb the product properly. Stripes can be marked out with masking tape.

3 These three materials are very easy to use. However, remember not to apply them too thickly. Apart from that anything goes: tone on tone, terracotta and brick, terracotta with brick and gold on top, terracotta with black or perhaps black or brick over gold. You will discover all kinds of possibilities as you go along, using this special technique which allows you lots of freedom.

HANDY TIPS!

If the pots are to be used as flowerpots, it's best to use slightly diluted acrylic paint. They can be turned into very decorative flowerpot-holders, utensil-holders or tidies.

To place a single flower in a pot, stick it into some florists' 'oasis'.

MOTIFS

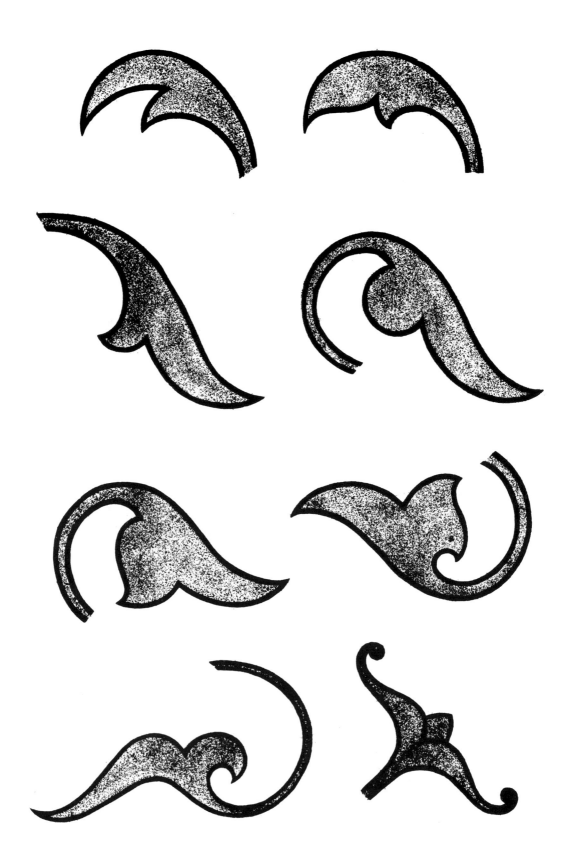

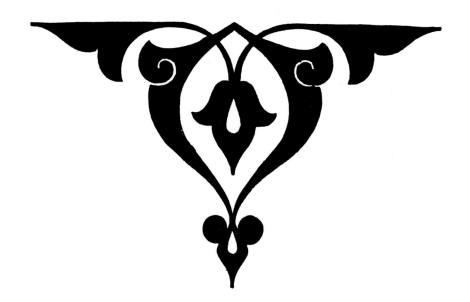

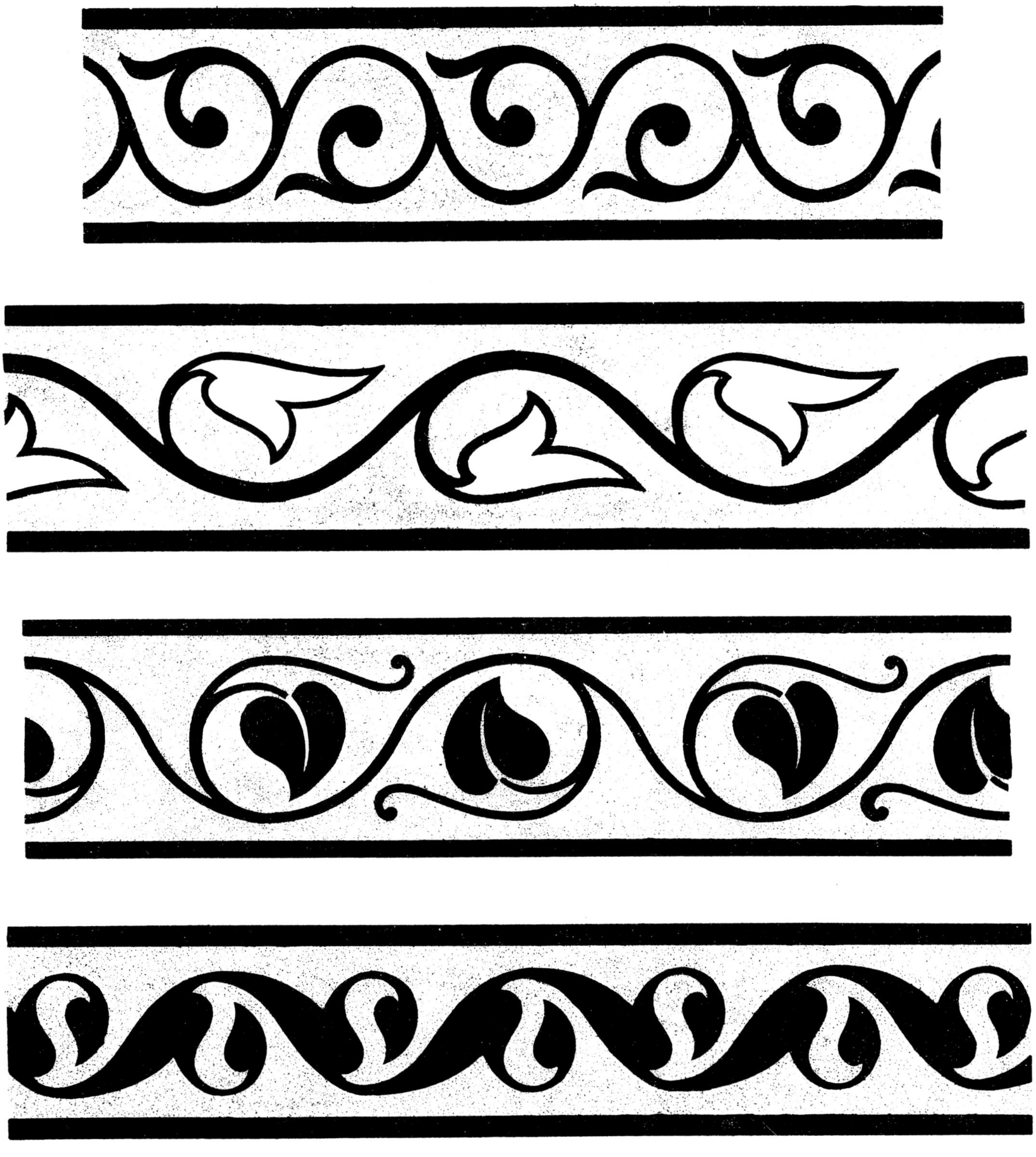

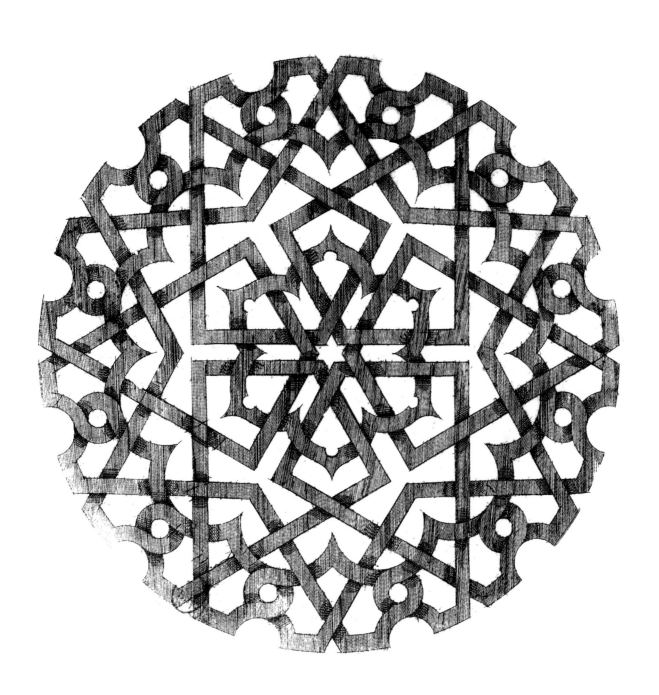

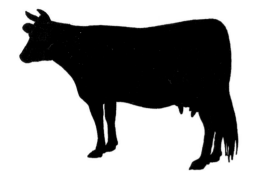

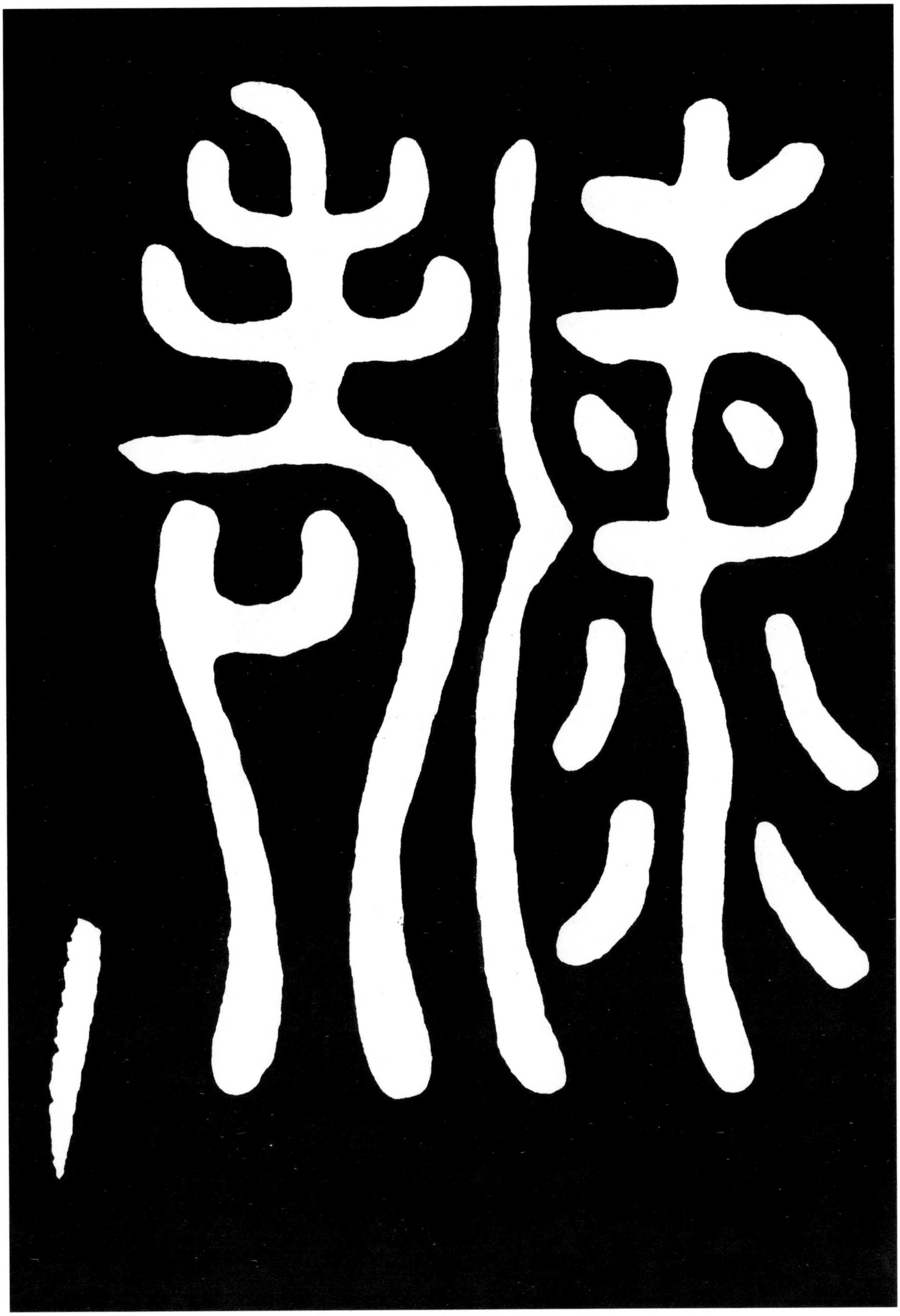